101 Cherry Recipes

by Carole Eberly

Cover by Kathi Terry

Copyright 1984, 1994 by **eberly press**

1004 W. Michigan Ave.

East Lansing, MI 48823

ISBN 0-932296-11-4

TABLE OF CONTENTS

Preserves
Jams
Sauces
and
Beverages

TART CHERRY JELLY

5 c. sugar
1 pkg. fruit pectin
3 c. cherry juice
1/2 c. water

Mix sugar and half the cherry juice. Mix pectin with water. Heat. Pour hot pectin mixture into remaining cherry juice. Let stand 15 minutes, then add sugar mixture. Stir until sugar is dissolved; pour into jars and let stand at room temperature for six hours. Refrigerate.

CHERRY JAM

2 c. cherries, chopped
1 pkg. pectin
4 c. sugar
1 c. water

Mix fruit and sugar. Boil pectin and water, stirring constantly. Remove from heat. Add cherries and stir for a few minutes. Pour into jars and seal.

MYSTERY JELLY

1 c. grape juice
1 3/4 c. blueberry juice
7 c. sugar
2 1/4 c. cherry juice
1 pkg. pectin

Combine juices and pectin, bring to a boil. Add sugar and boil for another minute. Remove from heat and stir for five minutes. Pour into hot jars and seal.

CHERRY MARMALADE

2 oranges
4 T lemon juice
1 qt. cherries, pitted
3 1/2 c. sugar

Peel orange, scrape white membrane from the peel and slice into slivers. Chop orange pulp and mix with peel. Measure orange mixture and add an equal amount of water. Boil, then simmer until peel is tender. Add cherries, lemon juice and sugar; cook rapidly until it reaches the jellying point. Pour into sterilized jars. Seal.

CHERRY BUTTER

Wash and pit cherries. Cook until soft, about 10 minutes. Press through a colander then through a strainer. Add 1 c. sugar for each cup pulp. Add 1 stick cinnamon and 1/8 t. salt for each 3 c. pulp. Boil rapidly, stirring constantly. Reduce heat as it cooks down. It will take from 3 to 5 hours to finish. To test for doneness pour some on a plate. No liquid should separate from the butter. Remove cinnamon and pour hot butter into sterilized jars.

BRANDIED CHERRIES

5 c. black cherries
1/2 c. brandy
2 c. sugar

Pit the cherries. Cook the pits in enough water to cover for 15 minutes. Reserve the liquid. Mix 2 c. liquid and 2 c. sugar and bring to a boil. Boil for 5 minutes. Add fruit and cook until cherries are tender, about 10 minutes. Pack fruit in jars. Cook syrup until it is thick - 222 degrees. Add 1/4 c. brandy to each jar, then fill with syrup. Make about 2 pints.

CHERRY-APRICOT SAUCE

Combine one cup apricot preserves and 1/2 cup maraschino cherries which have been quartered. That's all there is to it.

CHERRY & CREAM DRESSING

2 eggs
1/8 t. salt
3 T. confectioners sugar
1/2 c. cherry juice
1/2 t. vanilla
1 c. whipping cream

Beat eggs and pour into top of a double boiler. Add sugar, salt and cherry juice, mix. Cook over hot water until the sauce will coat a spoon. Cool, add vanilla. When ready to serve whip cream and fold in. Best when served cold.

CHERRY CAKE FILLING

1 c. dried cherries
1 c. water
2/3 c. sugar
1/8 t. salt
1 c. light corn syrup
1 egg, lightly beaten
1 t. vanilla

In a double boiler, cook cherries, water, sugar, salt and corn syrup together until cherries are soft. Remove from heat and add the egg. Return to heat and cook, stirring constantly, until the mixture coats a spoon. Cool and add vanilla.

TRIPLE-CHERRY SAUCE

2 c. light sweet cherries
2 c. sour cherries
2 c. black cherries
3 T. lemon juice
6 c. sugar

Pit, then measure cherries. Chop coarsely. Simmer about 5 minutes to soften. Add sugar and lemon juice. Cook until thickened, about 15 to 20 minutes. Don't over-cook! Pour into hot jars.

CHERRY ICING

2 c. cherries
Powdered sugar (to taste)
4 egg whites
1/8 t. salt

Crush cherries. Add powdered sugar to taste - set aside until the sugar is dissolved. Drain pulp and add egg whites and salt beaten until stiff but not dry. Beat in 1/4 c. powdered sugar. Add fruit pulp and spread on cake.

CHERRY JAM FILLING

Whip 1/2 c. cream until stiff. Fold in 1/2 c. cherry jam. Spread thickly between cake layers.

BRANDIED DESERT FRUITS

    1 lb. light brown sugar
    3 c. water
    1 1/2 lbs. raisins
    1 c. dried cherries
    1/2 c. almonds
    6 oz. dried apricots
    1 pkg. dates
    1 c. brandy

Combine sugar and water and bring to a boil. Reduce heat and simmer for 5 minutes. Add brandy after mixture has cooled slightly. Put fruits and nuts in jars and cover with the syrup mixture.

FRESH BLACK CHERRY SYRUP

2 c. black cherries, pitted
1/2 c. water
1/2 c. sugar
1 t. vanilla

Boil cherries and water for 10 minutes. Strain and press through a sieve.
Add sugar to juice and pulp. Boil 5 to 8 minutes more. Cool; add vanilla.
Serve hot or cold.

CHERRY SAUCE

3/4 c. cherry juice
1/2 c. sugar
1/8 t. salt
1 1/2 t. cornstarch
1/2 c. sour cherries
1 T butter
1 T. lemon juice

Stir cherry juice into mixture of sugar, salt and cornstarch. Cook over low heat for 5 minutes, stirring constantly. Add cherries, butter and lemon juice. Serve hot.

CHOCOLATE CHERRY SAUCE

1 1-oz. square unsweetened chocolate
1/4 c. water
12 regular size marshmallows
1/3 c. dried cherries

Combine all ingredients in a saucepan and cook over medium heat until marshmallows and chocolate are melted. Serve warm over ice cream.

MAPLE CHERRY GRANOLA

4 c. rolled oats
1 c. chopped walnuts
1 c. coconut
1/2 t. salt
1/4 c. maple syrup
1/4 c. cooking oil
1 c. dried cherries

Mix oats, nuts, coconut and salt together. Mix maple syrup and oil together; add to the oat mixture. Put the mixture on a cookie sheet and spread it out. Bake at 375 degrees for about 40 minutes, stirring often. After removing from oven, add cherries.

SPICED CHERRY SAUCE

1 package frozen tart cherries
1/2 c. sugar
1/4 t. allspice
1/4 t. cinnamon
1 c. light corn syrup
3 1/2 T. lemon juice
1/4 ground cloves
1/4 t. vanilla

Drain cherries, saving juice. Combine juice with everything but vanilla and bring to a boil. Simmer 15 minutes, stirring often. Remove from heat; add cherries and vanilla.

CHERRY LEMONADE PUNCH

1 qt. cherry juice
1 16-oz. bottle lemon soda
1 6-oz. can frozen lemonade

Mix cherry juice and lemonade together. Slowly add bottle of lemon soda. Serve over ice.

CHERRY SHAKE

1 can cherry pie filling
1 c. milk
1 qt. ice cream
4 t. lemon juice

Place all ingredients in a blender and mix. Add more milk if too thick.

EXTRACTING CHERRY JUICE

For both red and black cherries: Wash and pit, put through a food chopper. Heat to 160 degrees. Drain and squeeze through a cloth bag. Strain.

CHERRY RELISH

2 c. cherries, pitted
1 t. cinnamon
1/2 c. honey
1 c. raisins
1/2 t. cloves
1/2 c. vinegar
1 c. pecans

Combine all ingredients but nuts. Cook slowly for an hour. Add pecans and cook three more minutes. Pour into hot sterilized jars. Seal and process.

PICKLED CHERRIES

2 qts. black cherries
24 whole cloves
1 stick cinnamon
2 1/4 c. vinegar
4 T. sugar

Tie spices in a bag, mix sugar and vinegar, add spices and cook for 5 minutes. Add cherries (with pits) and cook slowly until tender. Let stand overnight. Remove spice bag. Place cherries in hot sterilized jars. Boil reserved spicy syrup until it thickens slightly. Pour hot over cherries; seal.

CHERRY STRAWBERRY SPREAD

2 1/2 c. black cherries, pitted
2 c. sliced strawberries
3 c. sugar
1/2 t. almond extract
1/4 c. lemon juice

Combine cherries, strawberries and sugar. Cook over low heat until sugar is dissolved. Boil 8 minutes while stirring. Add lemon juice and almond extract; continue to boil until it reaches the jellying point. Pour into jars.

CHERRY-RASPBERRY CONSERVE

6 c. sour cherries, pitted
3 c. sugar
2 c. black raspberries

Combine all ingredients and cook until thick, about 20 minutes. Stir often. Pour into sterilized, hot jars.

BLACK CHERRY BOUNCE

3 lbs. black cherries
1 T. allspice
1 T. cloves
1 lb. sugar
1 cinnamon stick
1 qt. whiskey

Wash cherries and remove stems. Put all ingredients in a large jar and stir. Cover and let stand for about two months. Strain.

RED CHERRY BOUNCE

2 qts. sour cherries
2 quarts whiskey
2 lbs. sugar

Mix all together and let stand in a covered jar or crock for at least two months. Stir once a week. Strain and bottle.

CHERRY NUT CAKE

1 1/2 c. oil
3 eggs
2 c. sugar
1 t. baking soda
chopped

1 1/2 t. vanilla
3 c. sifted flour
3 c. cherries,
pitted
1 c. pecans,

Mix oil, eggs and sugar together. Add baking soda, vanilla and the flour. Fold in cherries (chop slightly) and nuts. Pour into an oiled bundt pan and bake at 300 degrees for about 1 1/2 hours.

For a brochure describing other **eberly press** books, please write to:

eberly press

1004 Michigan Ave.

East Lansing, MI 48823

Breads and Salads

Cherry trees originated in the Far East and were cultivated by the Romans and the Greeks. The fruit was grown in America in the early 1600s by the first colonists who brought the cherry with them across the Atlantic Ocean.

One quart of cherries weighs about two pounds. One quart equals about 6 cups, unpitted, and 4 cups pitted.

To pit cherries use this tool made from a large hairpin and a red rubber eraser. Stick the hairpin into one end of the eraser. The eraser is the tool's "handle" and the loop in the hairpin is just the right size to pop the pits out.

CHERRY OATMEAL BREAD

2 c. sifted flour
3 t. baking powder
1/2 t. salt
1/2 t. baking soda
3/4 c. sugar
1 c. rolled oats
2 eggs
1/4 c. oil
1 c. milk
1 c. dried cherries

Sift together flour, baking powder, salt, soda and sugar. Stir in rolled oats. Beat eggs, add oil and milk. Add to dry ingredients and mix well. Add cherries last and pour into greased loaf pan. Bake at 350 degrees for about an hour.

CHERRY BANANA BREAD

1/2 c. dried cherries
1 c. boiling water
3/4 c. sugar
1/4 c. butter
2 eggs
2 c. sifted flour
2 t. baking powder
1/4 t. salt
1 1/2 c. bananas
1 t. almond extract

Boil cherries in water for 5 minutes. Mix sugar, butter and eggs well. Sift flour, baking powder and salt together, add to sugar mixture. Stir in cherries, bananas and extract. Bake in a well greased loaf pan for about an hour at 350 degrees.

CHERRY KUCHEN

2 1/2 c. flour
3/4 c. sugar, divided
1/2 t. salt
1 pkg. dry yeast
1/2 c. milk
1/4 c. water
1/2 c. butter, divided
1 egg
4 c. cherries, pitted
2 t. cinnamon

Mix 3/4 c. flour, 2 T. sugar, salt and yeast. Combine milk, water and 1/4 c. butter in a saucepan. Warm, then add to dry ingredients. Add egg and more flour, enough to make a stiff batter. Cover and let rise until doubled. Punch down and pour into two 9-inch cake pans. Top with cherries. Mix remaining sugar, butter and cinnamon together and sprinkle over fruit. Let rise again until doubled. Bake at 375 degrees for about 25 minutes.

CHERRY MUFFINS

2 c. flour
1/4 c. sugar
2 1/2 t. baking powder
1/2 t. salt
1 egg
1 c. milk
1/3 c. shortening
1 c. black cherries, pitted

Sift together flour, sugar, baking powder and salt. Mix egg, milk and shortening; combine with dry ingredients. Chop up cherries a little and add to the batter. Fill greased muffin pans 2/3 full and bake at 400 degrees for about 12 minutes.

CHERRY CRUMB MUFFINS

2 c. flour
3 t. baking powder
1/2 c. sugar
1/4 t. salt
1 1/4 c. cherries, pitted
1 egg
1/4 c. oil
1 c. milk
1/4 c. butter
1/3 c. brown sugar
1/2 t. cinnamon
1/2 c. flour

Sift flour, baking powder, sugar and salt together. Add the cherries (chop a little first). Beat egg, oil and milk together then add to dry ingredients. Fill muffin cups 2/3 full with batter. Melt butter, add brown sugar, cinnamon and 1/2 c. flour. Sprinkle this mixture over the batter. Bake at 375 degrees for about 30 minutes.

BLACK CHERRY BISCUITS

2 c. flour
3/4 t. salt
1 T. baking powder
3/4 c. shortening
1/2 t. baking soda
1 c. buttermilk
24 black cherries, pitted
24 small sugar cubes

Sift flour with salt and baking powder; mix in 1/4 c. shortening, baking soda and the buttermilk. Knead dough. Roll out dough to about 1/2-inch thickness and cut in biscuit-size rounds. Place on a well-greased pan. Press a cherry and a sugar cube in each. Let rise 15 minutes and bake at 450 degrees for about 15 minutes.

CHERRY BRAN MUFFINS

1 egg
1/2 c. milk
1/4 c. oil
2 c. bran cereal
1 c. sour cherries, pitted
1 c. sifted flour
1/2 c. sugar
2 t. baking powder
1/8 t. salt
1/2 t. nutmeg

Combine egg, milk and oil. Stir in cereal and cherries. Sift flour, sugar, baking powder, salt and nutmeg. Add to egg mixture. Fill muffin cups 2/3 full and bake at 400 degrees for about 20 minutes.

CHERRY GRIDDLECAKES

1 1/2 c. dried cherries
1/4 c. sugar
3 t. baking powder
1 c. milk
2 c. sifted flour
1/2 t. salt
2 eggs
1/4 c. shortening

Sift dry ingredients together. Beat eggs, mix in milk and add shortening.
Add to dry ingredients. Fold in cherries. Serves 4 to 6.

FRESH CHERRY WAFFLES

2 c. flour
2 1/2 t. baking powder
1/4 t. salt
1 T. sugar
2 eggs, separated
1 1/4 c. milk
2 T. oil
1 1/2 c. sour cherries, pitted

Sift together flour, baking powder, salt and sugar. Mix egg yolks, milk and oil. Add to dry ingredients and mix. Beat egg whites and fold in along with cherries. Makes about a dozen waffles. Serve with cherry sauce!

CHERRY-OLIVE SALAD

1 6-oz. pkg. lime gelatin
Black cherry juice
1/2 c. lemon juice
1/3 c. chopped pecans
1 16-oz. can black cherries
1 3-oz. bottle olives

Dissolve gelatin in 3 c. boiling liquid (use cherry and lemon juice - make up difference with water). Chill until partially set. Add cherries, nuts and olives. Pour into a mold and chill until set.

CHERRY-COLA MOLD

1 8-oz. pkg. cream cheese
1/4 c. mayonnaise
1 3-oz. pkg. cherry gelatin
1 3-oz. pkg. strawberry gelatin
1 c. boiling water
1 13-oz. can pineapple chunks
1 12-oz. bottle cola soda
1 16-oz. can sweet cherries
1 c. chopped nuts

Blend cream cheese and mayonnaise, dissolve gelatins in water and then add to cheese mixture. Drain pineapple and cherries saving 1 1/2 c. syrup. Add syrup and cola to gelatin and chill. Once set, add cherries, nuts and pineapple. Pour into mold and chill until well set.

WHITE CHERRY SALAD

1 egg white
1 pt. whipping cream
1 can white cherries
1/2 lb. slivered almonds
Juice of 1/2 lemon
Chopped almonds
1/2 lb. miniature marshmallows

Beat egg white and cream together. Add other ingredients slowly, whipping as you go. Pour into a mold and chill until well set. Unmold and garnish with chopped almonds.

FRUIT MELANGE

1 can black cherries
1 can pineapple chunks
1 pt. strawberries
1 banana
1/2 c. orange marmalade
1/4 c. hot water
1/2 T. chopped candied ginger

Layer fruits (except banana) in a large glass bowl. Combine marmalade, hot water and ginger. Pour over fruit then chill. When ready to serve garnish with sliced banana.

CRANBERRY CHERRY SALAD

1 3-oz. pkg. cherry gelatin
1 3-oz. pkg. lemon gelatin
1 1/2 c. boiling water
1 16-oz. pkg. frozen cherries
1 16-oz. can jellied cranberry sauce
1 12-oz. bottle lemon-lime soda

Dissolve the two gelatins in the water. Stir in frozen cherries. Mash cranberry sauce with a fork and then mix in. Chill until slightly thickened and then add soda. Chill until well set.

CHERRY JUBILEE MOLD

1 can black cherries
2 3-oz. pkgs. cherry gelatin
1/2 c. cream sherry
1 3-oz. pkg. cream cheese
Chopped nuts
1 can pear halves

Drain cherries saving syrup. Take syrup and add enough water to make three cups. Mix gelatin and liquid until gelatin dissolves. Stir in sherry. Chill until it sets a little. Fold in cherries and pour into the mold. Form cream cheese into small balls which will about fill cavity in the pear. Roll in nuts and place in pears. When mold is turned out, decorate with pears and lettuce leaves.

CHILLED FRUIT COMPOTE

1/2 c. raisins
1/2 c. dried prunes
2 c. cold water
1/2 c. apricots
1 cinnamon stick
2 apples, peeled & sliced
2 pears, peeled & sliced
2 c. sour cherries
1 3-oz. pkg. cherry gelatin
1 c. boiling water

In a large saucepan, soak the dried fruit with 2 c. cold water for about an hour. Add cinnamon and peeled and sliced apples and pears. Simmer for about 10 minutes or until fruit is tender. Add cherries, juice and all, and bring to a boil. Dissolve gelatin in boiling water and then add to fruit. Chill.

ALL DAY SALAD

1 can pineapple chunks
1 can sweet cherries
3 egg yolks
2 1/2 T. vinegar
3 T. sugar
1/4 t. salt
1 T. butter
2 oranges, peeled & sliced
2 c. miniature marshmallows
1 c. whipping cream, whipped

Drain pineapple and cherries, save 2 T. syrup from each. In top of a double boiler, beat egg yolks, add syrups, vinegar, sugar, salt and butter. Place over hot water and, stirring constantly, cook slowly until it thickens slightly. Cool. Combine sliced orange, pineapple, cherries and marshmallows and egg mixture. Mix gently. Fold in whipped cream. Pour into a serving dish and chill for a whole day.

CHERRY-MINCEMEAT MOLD

1 can sweet cherries
2 3-oz. pkgs. cherry gelatin
2 c. boiling water
2 1/2 T. lemon juice
1/2 c. mincemeat
1/2 c. diced apple
1/2 c. chopped pecans
1/4 t. cinnamon

Drain cherries, save juice. Dissolve gelatin in the boiling water. Add water to cherry juice until you have 2 3/4 c. liquid. Add to the gelatin. Add lemon juice. Chill until thickened and fold in cherries, mincemeat, apple, pecans and cinnamon. Pour into mold, chill.

Main Dishes

CHERRY CHICKEN

6-8 chicken breasts, split
Garlic salt
Paprika
1 can sour cherries
1/2 c. sugar
1 T. flour
Dash salt
1 orange, peeled, sliced
1/2 c. almonds
1/3 c. sherry

Bone breasts. Sprinkle with garlic salt and paprika. Bake at 400 degrees for about 25 minutes. Pour cherries into a saucepan, saving 1/2 c. juice. Add sugar. Mix 1 T. flour with the juice. Mix into cherries with a dash of salt. Heat until it thickens. Add orange, almonds and sherry. Place chicken in sauce; simmer until all is hot. Serve.

HAM WITH CHERRY SAUCE

Canned ham
1 10-oz. jar apple jelly
1 T. mustard
1/3 c. pineapple juice
3 T. dry wine
1 can cherry pie filling
1/2 c. raisins

Cook ham according to directions on the can. About a half hour before ham is done, pour 1/3 of the following glaze over ham, spooning on more every 10 minutes. Combine jelly, mustard and pineapple juice with wine. Heat to boiling; simmer 3 minutes. Once ham is done, mix remaining glaze with pie filling and raisins. Heat to boiling. Spoon over ham.

CHICKEN & CHERRIES

1/3 c. flour
1 1/2 t. salt
1/2 t. paprika
1/4 t. garlic salt
3 chicken breasts
1/4 c. butter
1 can black cherries
1 c. sauterne

Combine flour, salt, paprika and garlic salt in a paper bag; add a couple of breasts which have been cut in half lengthwise and shake. Melt butter in skillet and brown the chicken. Add cherries; pour the sauterne over the top. Simmer, covered, about 35 minutes.

FRESH FRUIT STUFFING

2 t. butter
1 c. celery
1 c. onion
1 1/2 t. salt
1/2 t. pepper
1/2 t. sage
1/2 t. thyme
7 c. bread cubes, dry
2 apples, peeled, chopped
1 c. dried cherries
1/2 c. pecans, chopped
2 eggs

Saute celery and onions. Stir in salt, pepper, sage and thyme. Mix bread, apples, cherries and nuts. Stir in the onion mixture and eggs. Mix. Stuff bird.

SWEET AND SOUR PORK CHOPS

6 pork chops
3 T. vinegar
1 T. cornstarch
1/4 t. salt
1 can black cherries
3 T. brown sugar
1 t. minced onion
1/4 t. dried dill weed

Brown chops, drain cherries, saving syrup. Mix remaining ingredients with syrup and pour over chops. Cover and simmer for about 30 minutes. Remove chops and add cherries to sauce remaining. Heat, then pour over chops.

PORK CHOPS & CHERRIES

4 pork chops
Salt & pepper to taste
1 16-oz. can tart cherries
1 T. vinegar
6 cloves
1/4 c. slivered almonds

Brown pork chops. Season with salt and pepper. Combine cherries, cherry juice, vinegar, cloves and almonds. Pour over chops and simmer covered for 30 minutes.

Dieter's Information:

Fresh sweet cherries - 3 1/2 oz. - 70 calories

Fresh sour cherries - 3 1/2 oz. - 58 calories

Maraschino cherries - 3 1/2 oz. - 116 calories

Pies

TRAVERSE CITY CHERRY PIE

Pastry for 2-crust, 9-inch pie
3 c. sour cherries, pitted
1 c. sugar
1/2 c. flour
1/4 t. almond extract
1/8 t. salt
1 1/2 T. butter

Mix cherries with sugar, flour, extract and salt. Pour into pie shell. Dot with butter and place top crust on. Bake at 425 degrees for 10 minutes and 350 degrees for an additional 30 minutes.

BLACK CHERRY BURGUNDY PIE

Baked 9-inch pastry shell
1 c. water
1/4 c. sugar
1 3-oz. pkg. cherry gelatin
2 c. black cherries, pitted
1 pt. vanilla ice cream
3 T. burgundy
1 t. lemon juice

Boil water; dissolve sugar and gelatin in it. Stir in cherries. Add ice cream by spoonfuls, stirring until melted. Add wine and lemon juice. Pour into pie shell and chill until set.

CHERRY CHEESE PIE I

1 graham cracker pie crust
1 pkg. cream cheese
1 t. sugar
1 c. powdered sugar
1 large carton whipped topping
1 16-oz. can sour cherries

Mix cheese, 1/2 carton topping and sugars until smooth. Pour into the pie shell and top with cherries. Put remaining topping on cherries. Chill.

CHERRY CHEESE PIE II

Pastry for 9-inch pie, unbaked
1 1/2 c. cottage cheese
1 T. flour
1/8 t. salt
1 c. cream
2/3 c. sugar
Grated rind of a lemon
Juice of the lemon
3 eggs, separated
1/2 c. cherry preserves

Combine mashed cottage cheese, flour and salt. Stir in cream, sugar, rind and the lemon juice. Whip egg whites until stiff and beat the egg yolks until thick. Add yolks to cheese mixture and fold in the whites. Spread pie shell with preserves. Add cheese mixture. Bake at 450 degrees for 10 minutes; reduce heat to 350 degrees for 45 minutes.

BLACK CHERRY CREAM PIE

Baked 9-inch pie shell
1 pkg. vanilla pudding
2 c. milk
3/4 c. black cherries
3 1/2 T. cherry gelatin
1/2 c. boiling water
1/2 c. water

Make pudding with milk. Chill; then pour into pie shell. Slice cherries in half and place on top of pudding. Dissolve gelatin and boiling water. Stir in 1/2 c. water. Chill until thickened. Spoon over cherries. Chill to set.

CHERRY CHIFFON PIE

Unbaked 8-inch pie shell
1 envelope unflavored gelatin
1/4 c. water
1 16-oz. can sour cherries, with juice
1/2 c. sugar
1/8 t. salt
1 T. lemon juice
1/2 c. whipping cream

Mix gelatin and water. Stir in cherries and juice with sugar, salt and lemon juice. Heat to boiling, stirring all the while. Chill until thickened. Whip cream and fold into cherry mixture. Pour into pie shell and chill.

CHERRY CUSTARD PIE

Pastry for 2-crust, 9-inch pie
2 eggs
3 T. milk
1 T. melted butter
1/8 t. salt
3 T. flour
1 1/2 c. sugar
1 t. nutmeg
3 c. tart cherries, pitted

Beat eggs slightly, add milk, butter and salt. Mix flour, sugar and nutmeg. Add to egg mixture. Add cherries. Pour into bottom pastry. Cover with top crust. Bake at 425 degrees for about 40 minutes.

CHERRY BRANDY PIE

Unbaked 9-inch pastry shell
1 qt. sour cherries, pitted
1 c. sugar
2 eggs
1/2 c. milk
1/2 c. cherry juice
1/8 t. salt
4 T. brandy
Nutmeg

Mix cherries and sugar and let stand. Beat 2 eggs; add milk and 1/2 c. juice drained from cherry mixture. Add salt and brandy. Place cherries in shell and pour egg mixture over top. Sprinkle with nutmeg. Bake at 450 degrees for 15 minutes; 325 degrees for an additional 30-45 minutes.

CHERRY APPLE PIE

Pastry for 2-crust 9-inch pie
4 large apples
6 T. butter, divided
1 c. sugar
2 T. flour
1/2 t. nutmeg
2 1/2 t. cinnamon
2 1/2 c. sour cherries, pitted

Pare, core and slice apples. Melt 2 T. butter and brush bottom of the shell.
Mix the dry ingredients. Place a layer of apple slices, then the dry mixture,
then cherries. Continue until all ingredients are used, finishing with apples.
Dot with butter and cover with top crust. Bake at 425 degrees for 10
minutes; 325 degrees for an additional 30-40 minutes.

CHERRY CREAM PIE

Baked 9-inch pie crust
1 can cherry pie filling
1 1/2 c. sour cream

Fill the crust by layering cherries and sour cream. Swirl mixture slightly, then refrigerate until set - about an hour.

CHERRY MERINGUE PIE

Unbaked 9-inch pie shell
3 eggs, separated
3/4 t. almond extract
1/4 c. melted butter
1/4 c. flour
1 c. sugar
1/8 t. salt
4 c. sour cherries, pitted
10 T. sugar
1 t. vinegar

Beat egg yolks. Add extract and butter. Sift dry ingredients. Stir in yolk mixture and cherries. Pour into pie shell and bake at 375 degrees for about 45 minutes. Top with: 3 egg whites, beaten stiff, adding the 10 T. sugar and 1 t. vinegar as you beat. Top pie and bake at 350 degrees for another 15 minutes.

TWO CHERRY PIE

Pastry for 9-inch, 2-crust pie
2 c. sour cherries, pitted
1 c. black cherries, pitted
3/4 c. sour cherry juice
1/2 c. black cherry juice
1/2 c. sugar
2 1/4 T. quick-cooking tapioca
2 T. cornstarch
1 t. lemon juice

Set cherries aside. Mix cherry juices, sugar, tapioca and cornstarch. Heat until thick. Cool. Stir cherries and lemon juice into the thickened juice. Pour into pie shell. Cover with top crust and bake at 425 degrees for about 30 minutes.

CHERRY NUT PIE

Baked 8-inch pie shell
1 16-oz. can sour cherries
1 3-oz. pkg. black cherry gelatin
1 c. boiling water
1/4 t. cinnamon
3/4 c. sugar
1/2 c. chopped nuts

Drain cherries, reserving 1/2 c. juice. Dissolve gelatin in water; add cherry juice. Add cinnamon and sugar. Chill. Add cherries and nuts; pour into the pie shell. Good with whipped cream!

CHERRY TURNOVERS

1 can sour cherries
1 1/2 T. cornstarch
1/3 c. sugar
1/4 t. salt
1/8 t. nutmeg
1/3 c. cherry juice
1 t. grated lemon rind
1 t. lemon juice
2 1/2 T. butter
2 c. flour
1/2 t. salt
1/3 c. ice water
2/3 c. butter

Drain cherries; reserve juice. Heat cornstarch, sugar, salt and nutmeg. Add reserved cherry juice, lemon juice and rind. Cook until thick and clear. Stir in 2 1/2 T. butter and cherries. Sift flour and salt, cut in 2/3 c. butter. Stir in ice water. Divide dough, roll out into 12x12-inch squares, cut each into 4 squares. Place a spoonful of cherry mixture on each small square and fold over to make a triangle, slit top. Bake at 425 degrees for about 20 minutes.

CHERRY JELLY PIE

Unbaked pie shell
1/4 c. butter
1 c. sugar
2 eggs
1 t. vanilla
3/4 c. cherry jelly
1 t. lemon juice
1 t. nutmeg
1 c. milk

Cream butter, add sugar, eggs, vanilla, jelly (beat first), lemon juice and nutmeg. Stir in milk, pour into pie shell and bake for 15 minutes at 450 degrees; reduce heat to 325 degrees for an additional 40 minutes.

CHERRY SOUR CREAM PIE

Unbaked 9-inch pie shell
2 eggs
1/2 c. sugar
1 c. sour cream
1 c. dried cherries
1/4 t. salt
1 t. cinnamon
1/4 t. nutmeg
1 t. lemon juice

Beat eggs slightly. Add sugar, sour cream, cherries, salt, cinnamon, nutmeg and lemon juice. Pour mixture into pie shell and bake at 450 degrees for 15 minutes. Reduce heat to 325 degrees and continue baking for about 40 minutes.

CHERRY RAISIN PIE

Pastry for 2-crust, 9-inch pie
2 c. sour cherries, pitted
1 c. raisins
1 1/2 c. sugar
1 T. cornstarch
3/4 t. cinnamon
1/8 t. salt
1/2 t. ground cloves
2 T. butter

Mix cherries and raisins, filling unbaked pie shell. Mix sugar, cornstarch and spices; sprinkle over fruit. Dot with butter and cover with top crust or lattice. Bake at 450 degrees for about 35 minutes.

Desserts

and

Gooey Things

CHERRY BAVARIAN

1 envelope unflavored gelatin
2/3 c. sugar, divided
1/8 t. salt
1 can sour cherries
2 eggs, separated
1/2 t. almond extract
1 c. whipping cream

Mix gelatin with 1/3 c. sugar and salt. Drain cherries and save the juice. Beat egg yolks. Add cherry juice and gelatin mixture. Heat in saucepan until gelatin dissolves. Add almond extract and cherries. Chill. Beat egg whites with remaining sugar. Whip cream and fold both egg whites and whipped cream into cherry mixture. Chill. Garnish with some reserved whipped cream.

CHERRY MOUSSE

2 pkgs. frozen cherries
2 pkgs. unflavored gelatin
3/4 c. sugar
1 t. lemon juice
Dash salt
4 egg whites
2 c. cream
2 c. crushed macaroons
2 T. almond liqueur

Puree cherries; add gelatin and cook over low heat until dissolved. Add 1/4 c. sugar, lemon juice and salt. Heat until sugar is dissolved. Chill about 30 minutes. Beat egg whites with 1/4 c. sugar until stiff. Fold fruit mixture into egg whites. Beat 1 1/2 c. cream to soft peaks and fold in. Mix macaroon crumbs with liqueur. Put half of the mousse in serving bowl; top with macaroons. Top with remaining half of the mousse and garnish with whipped cream.

CHOCOLATE CHERRY CREAM

2 c. whipping cream
1/4 c. sugar
1 T. vanilla
4-oz. sweet chocolate, grated
3 c. black cherries, pitted

Whip cream with the sugar and vanilla. Add chocolate and mix. Fold cherries into cream and spoon into serving dishes. Chill.

CHERRY SHORTCAKE

2 c. sifted flour
2 T. sugar
2 1/4 t. baking powder
1/4 t. salt
1/2 c. butter
1 egg
1/2 c. milk
1 c. tart cherries
Sugar

Sift together flour, sugar, baking powder and salt; cut in butter. Mix in egg and milk. Divide dough in half and place half in an 8-inch round cake pan. Top with cherries (sweetened to taste). Roll remaining dough to an 8-inch circle and place over the cherries. Sprinkle with 2 t. sugar and bake at 400 degrees for about 25 minutes. Serve with cherry sauce (see below).

CHERRY SHORTCAKE SAUCE

1/4 c. sugar
1 1/2 T. cornstarch
1 c. water
1 c. cherries
1 T. lemon juice
1/4 c. butter

In a saucepan, combine the sugar, cornstarch and water; heat to a boil. Add remaining cherries and cook for 3 more minutes. Remove from heat and stir in lemon juice and butter. Pour over servings of shortcake.

CHERRY ANGEL PUDDING DELIGHT

8 c. 1/2-inch angel food cake cubes
1 can cherry pie filling
1 package instant vanilla pudding
1 1/2 c. milk
1 c. sour cream

Place half cake cubes in a 9x9-inch pan. Cover with 2/3 of cherries. Top with remaining cake. Combine pudding mix, milk and sour cream; beat until smooth. Pour over cake; chill until set. Before serving, garnish with remaining cherries.

CHERRY CAKE

1 pkg. yellow cake mix
3/4 c. cooking oil
4 eggs
1 pkg. frozen cherries
1 3-oz. pkg. cherry gelatin
1 c. chopped nuts
2 t. flour

Mix all ingredients and beat well. Pour into an angel food cake pan and bake at 350 degrees for about 45 minutes.

CHERRY JAM CAKE

1 c. brown sugar
1/2 c. butter
1 c. cherry jam
1 c. bananas
2 c. sifted flour
1/4 t. cloves
1/4 t. nutmeg
1/2 t. cinnamon
1 t. baking powder
1/2 c. buttermilk
1 t. baking soda
2 eggs
1 c. chopped nuts

Cream sugar and butter, add jam and bananas. Sift flour with spices and baking powder. Mix buttermilk with baking soda and add both flour and buttermilk mixtures to creamed butter. Add eggs and nuts; mix well. Pour into a 9x13-inch greased pan and bake at 350 degrees for about 40 minutes.

CHERRY CHIP FRUITCAKE

3 eggs
1 c. sugar
1 1/2 c. sifted flour
1 1/2 t. baking powder
1/4 t. salt
1 c. semisweet chocolate pieces
2 c. pecans
1 8-oz. pkg. dates
1 c. candied cherries

Beat eggs; add sugar. Sift flour, baking powder and salt. Mix with chocolate, pecans, dates and cherries. Fold in egg mixture. Pour into a greased loaf pan and bake at 325 degrees for about an hour. Place a pan of water in oven while baking.

CHERRY PUDDING

2 T. butter
2 c. sugar, divided
2 eggs
2 c. sifted flour
2 t. baking powder
1/4 t. salt
1 c. milk
1 can sour cherries
1 c. water

Mix butter and 1/2 cup sugar. Beat in the eggs. Sift dry ingredients together and add along with milk to sugar and eggs. Pour into a greased 9-inch pan. Drain cherries; combine juice and water; bring to a boil. Sprinkle cherries over batter and cover with remaining sugar. Pour boiling liquid over top. Bake in a 375 degree oven for about 45 minutes.

CHERRY ROLL-UP

1 c. biscuit mix
2 t. butter
1/4 c. cream
1 c. sour cherries, pitted
2 T. diced candied lemon peel
Cherry sauce

Mix biscuit mix and butter. Add cream, stir well. Turn out and knead slightly; roll into a rectangle 1/4-inch thick. Brush with a little melted butter, then top with cherries and lemon peel (sweeten the cherries, if you wish). Roll up dough like a jelly roll, brush with butter and bake at 400 degrees for about 20 minutes. Serve with cherry sauce.

CHERRY PLUMP

1 c. sifted flour
2 T. sugar
2 t. baking powder
1/4 t. salt
1 T. butter
2 1/2 c. fresh cherries
1/3 c. sugar
Dash salt
1 T. lemon juice
1/2 c. milk

Sift together flour, 2 T. sugar, baking powder and salt. Cut in butter. Using a heavy saucepan, bring cherries, 1/3 c. sugar, salt and 1 c. water to a boil. Cover and simmer for about 6 minutes. Add lemon juice. Add milk to dry ingredients and stir. Add dough to hot cherry mixture in spoonfuls, trying to keep dumplings from blending together. Cover and cook over low heat for about 10 more minutes. Serve with hot cream!

CHERRY CREAM-CHEESE FOLDOVERS

8-oz. pkg. cream cheese
1 c. butter
2 c. sifted flour
1/4 t. salt
Powdered sugar
Cherry jam

Cream cheese and butter. Sift together flour and salt. Mix the two together and chill. Roll to 1/8-inch thickness, sprinkle with a little powdered sugar and cut in tart-sized squares. Spread with the jam and fold over. Seal edges. Bake at 375 degrees for about 15 minutes. Decorate with a sprinkle of sugar.

ENERGY BARS

2 c. rolled oats
3 c. miniature marshmallows
1/2 c. chunky peanut butter
1/4 c. honey
3 T. butter
1 c. dried cherries

Toast oats in 350 degrees oven about 15 minutes. Melt marshmallows, peanut butter, honey and butter over low heat; stir constantly. Stir in oats and cherries; spread in a 9-inch square baking pan and chill until firm.

CHERRY BARS

1/2 c. butter
1 1/4 c. brown sugar
1 c. flour
1/4 t. salt
1/2 t. baking powder
1 6-oz. pkg. candied cherries
2 egg whites
1/2 t. cream of tartar
1/4 t. baking powder

Cream the butter and 1/4 c. brown sugar. Sift flour, salt and baking powder; mix in. Pat into greased 8x8-inch pan. Bake at 350 degrees for 10 minutes. Place cherries on top of baked mixture. Beat egg whites with 1/4 t. baking powder and cream of tartar. Beat in remaining brown sugar. Spread over cherries. Bake at 350 degrees until lightly browned.

CHERRY UPSIDE-DOWN CAKE

1 c. butter, divided
1/2 c. light brown sugar
1 lb. sour cherries, pitted
2 t. grated lemon peel
1/2 c. sugar
1 egg
1 1/2 c. sifted flour
2 1/2 t. baking powder
1/4 t. salt
1/2 c. milk

Melt 1/2 c. butter in a 9-inch square pan. Sprinkle with brown sugar. Spoon drained cherries over sugar. Sprinkle with lemon peel. Cream 1/2 c. butter with the 1/2 c. sugar, egg. Sift flour with baking powder and salt. Mix in milk and butter mixture. Pour over cherries. Bake at 375 degrees for 30 minutes. Serve with cherry sauce.

CHERRY CHOCOLATE CLUSTERS

1 6-oz. pkg. chocolate chips
1/4 c. light corn syrup
2 t. vanilla
2 T. powdered sugar
2 c. dried cherries

Combine chips and syrup in the top of a double boiler. Stir until chocolate is melted. Remove from heat and add vanilla, sugar and cherries. Drop by spoonfuls on to buttered cookie sheet. Chill.

WHEAT CHERRY CHOCOLATE CHIP COOKIES

1 1/2 c. butter
1 1/2 c. brown sugar
1 1/2 c. sugar
2 1/2 t. vanilla
4 eggs
2 1/2 c. flour
2 1/2 c. whole wheat flour
1/2 t. salt
2 t. baking soda
1 c. dried cherries
1 c. chopped nuts
1 12-oz. pkg. chocolate chips

Beat butter until soft, adding sugar, vanilla, eggs, flour and salt until well mixed. Mix baking soda with 2 T. hot water and add to mixture along with fruit, nuts and chocolate chips. Drop on greased cookie sheet in walnut sized balls, flatten. Bake at 350 degrees for about 10 minutes. Makes 48 cookies (if you don't eat any dough!).

CHERRY-FILLED OATMEAL COOKIES

1/2 c. shortening
1 c. sugar
2 c. flour
1 t. baking soda
1/2 t. salt
1/2 c. sour milk
2 c. oatmeal

Cream the shortening; add sugar, beat. Sift flour, soda and salt. Add to batter with milk. Add oatmeal. Roll dough to 1/8-inch thickness and cut with a round cutter. Place a teaspoon of the filling in the center and cover with remaining round. Seal edges with a fork. Bake at 375 degrees for about 10 minutes.

FILLING

Place 1/2 lb. dried cherries, 1 c. water and 1/2 c. brown sugar in a saucepan and cook until mixture thickens, stirring until the sugar is dissolved. Add 1 T. lemon juice and 1 t. grated lemon rind.

CHRISTMAS CHERRY FUDGE

3 c. sugar
1 1/2 c. cream
1 c. light corn syrup
1 t. salt
3 t. vanilla
1 1/2 c. halved candied cherries
1 1/2 c.walnuts
1 c. diced candied pineapple
1 1/2 c. Brazil nuts
2 c. pecans

Combine sugar, cream, corn syrup and salt. Cook over medium heat until sugar is dissolved. Cook to soft ball stage (236 degrees). Remove from heat and add vanilla. Beat with an electric mixer until creamy - about 10 minutes. Mix in remaining ingredients and pour into pan. Chill.

CHERRY NUT CHOCOLATE STICKS

1 c. brown sugar
1 c. light corn syrup
1 1/t t. salt
1 1/2 c. cream
3 c. dried cherries
1 c. chopped pecans
2 T. vanilla
1 1/2 lbs. chocolate for dipping

Combine sugar, corn syrup, salt and cream. Cook over medium heat to firm ball stage (247 degrees). Remove from heat, add cherries, nuts and vanilla. Pour into a 9-inch square pan that has been oiled and dusted with flour. Cool. Cut in narrow bars and dip in melted chocolate.

CHERRY WHITE FUDGE

1 3-oz. pkg. cream cheese
1/2 t. almond extract
1/2 c. dried cherries
2 1/2 c. powdered sugar
1/8 t. salt

Beat cream cheese until smooth. Blend in remaining ingredients. Press into pan and chill well.

CHERRY FUDGE

1 3-oz. pkg. cherry gelatin
3 1/2 c. sugar
1/2 t. baking soda
1 1/2 c. milk
1/2 c. butter
3/4 c. candied cherries
1/2 c. chopped pecans

Combine gelatin, sugar, baking soda and milk. Cook over medium heat to soft ball stage (236 degrees). Remove from heat and add butter. Pour onto a buttered baking dish and stir until gloss is gone. Stir in cherries and nuts. Pat into an 8-inch square pan and chill.

CHERRY SKILLET CAKE

1/3 c. butter
2 c. sugar, divided
1 c. chopped nuts
2 c. sour cherries
2/3 c. shortening
2 eggs
2 1/2 c. flour
3 t. baking powder
1/4 t. salt
2 t. vanilla
2/3 c. milk

Use an oven-proof 10-inch skillet. Melt butter in skillet, sprinkle 1/2 c. sugar over butter and add nuts and cherries. Cream shortening with 1 1/2 c. sugar, add eggs. Sift flour with baking powder, salt. Add vanilla and dry ingredients to shortening mixture. Add milk. Pour batter over cherry mixture in skillet. Bake at 350 degrees for about 50 minutes. Serve with cherry sauce.

CHERRY CRUMB CAKE

2 c. sifted flour
2 1/2 t. baking powder
1/4 t. salt
1/4 c. butter
3/4 c. sugar
1 egg
1/2 c. milk
2 c. cherries

Sift together flour, baking powder and salt. Cream butter with the sugar.
Add egg and milk and beat until smooth. Add dry ingredients. Fold in
cherries. Pour into a 9-inch square pan and top with crumb topping. Bake at
375 degrees for about 40 minutes.

CRUMB TOPPING

1/2 c. sugar
1 t. cinnamon
1/4 c. flour
1/4 c. butter

Mix together all dry ingredients. Cut in butter.